D1141264

BAINTE DEN STOC

WITHDRAWN FROM DLR LIBRARIES STOCK

Caring for our Earth

Written by Sally Hewitt

W

FRANKLIN WATTS

LONDON·SYDNEY

First published in 2009 by Franklin Watts
338 Euston Road, London NW1 3BH

Franklin Watts Australia
Hachette Children's Books
Level 17/207 Kent Street, Sydney NSW 2000

Copyright © Franklin Watts 2009

Editor: Katie Dicker
Art Direction: Dibakar Acharjee (Q2AMedia)
Designer: Tarang Saggar (Q2AMedia)
Picture researcher: Kamal Kumar (Q2AMedia)
Craft models made by: Jyotsna Julka (Q2AMedia),
Shweta Nigam (Q2AMedia)
Photography: Tarang Saggar (Q2AMedia)

Picture credits:
t=top b=bottom c=centre l=left r=right

Cover: Stuart O'Sullivan/Taxi/Getty Images.
Title: Noam Armonn/Shutterstock
Insides: Kwest/Shutterstock: 6, Monika
Adamczyk/Dreamstime: 7t, Robyn Mackenzie/123rf:
7b, Tomasz Szymanski/Shutterstock: 9tr, Ariel
Skelley/Corbis:9br, Difydave Difydave/Istockphoto:
9bl, Richard Hutchings/Corbis: 10, Rolf
Bruderer/Corbis: 12, Bonniej Graphic
Design/Istockphoto: 13t, OnlyVectors/Shutterstock:
13b, Bob Sacha/Corbis: 14, Timeflight/Istockphoto:
15tr, Index Stock Imagery/Photolibrary: 15cr, Shin
Henmi/Ailead/Amana images/Getty Images: 16,
Lawrence Migdale/Photo Researchers/Photolibrary:
17tr, Morgan Lane Photography/Shutterstock: 18,
Audaxl/Istockphoto: 19tr, Phil Date/123rf: 19cl,
Konstantin Remizov/Shutterstock: 19cr, Noam
Armonn/Shutterstock: 19br, Dean Conger/Corbis: 20,
Gregory James Van Raalte/Shutterstock: 22, Tadija
Savic/123rf: 23tr, Harvey Hudson/Fotolia: 23c,
Charles Mccarthy/Dreamstime: 23bl, Carlos
Caetano/Shutterstock: 23br, Momatiuk-
Eastcott/Corbis: 24, Visuals Unlimited/Corbis: 25tl,
Jose Manuel Gelpi/Fotolia: 25br, Tim
Jenner/Dreamstime: 25bl, Klaus
Rademaker/Dreamstime: 26.
Q2AMedia Image Bank: Imprint page, Contents page,
17, 21, 23, 27.
Q2AMedia Art Bank: 8, 11, 15.

With thanks to our model Shruti Aggarwal.

Every attempt has been made to clear copyright.
Should there be any inadvertent omission please
apply to the publisher for rectification.

ISBN 978 0 7496 8764 9

Dewey Classification: 304.2

A CIP catalogue record for this book
is available from the British Library

Printed in China

Franklin Watts is a division of Hachette Children's
Books, an Hachette UK company.
www.hachette.co.uk

Leabharlanna Dhún Laoghaire · Ráth An Dúin

Contents

Planet Earth

Earth, the planet we live on, is amazing. Animals and plants live almost everywhere. Hills and valleys are covered in flowers, deep seas are full of fish and people live in big cities and tiny villages.

Earth is the only planet we know of that has air and water and is the right temperature to support life.

Careful living

Some of the things we do in our daily lives can harm the planet and the plants and animals that live here. But there are many other things we can do to take care of planet Earth.

Air

All living things need air to survive. Animals, including people, breathe in oxygen, a gas in the air, and breathe out the gas carbon dioxide. Plants take in carbon dioxide and give out oxygen.

Global warming

Earth is kept warm by a layer of gases that traps heat from the Sun. When **fossil fuels** are burned, they release carbon dioxide into the air. This traps even more heat from the Sun. We call this '**global warming**'.

Trees help to keep the air full of oxygen for us to breathe. We should plant trees to replace those we use.

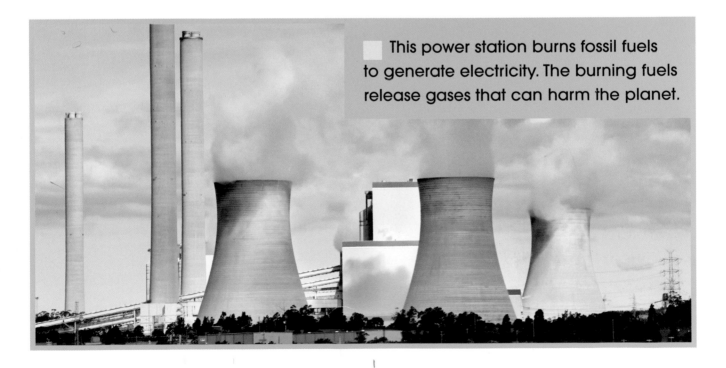

This power station burns fossil fuels to generate electricity. The burning fuels release gases that can harm the planet.

Water

All life on Earth depends on water. About three-quarters of the planet is covered in water, but most of this is salty sea water we can't drink. Only a small amount is fresh water.

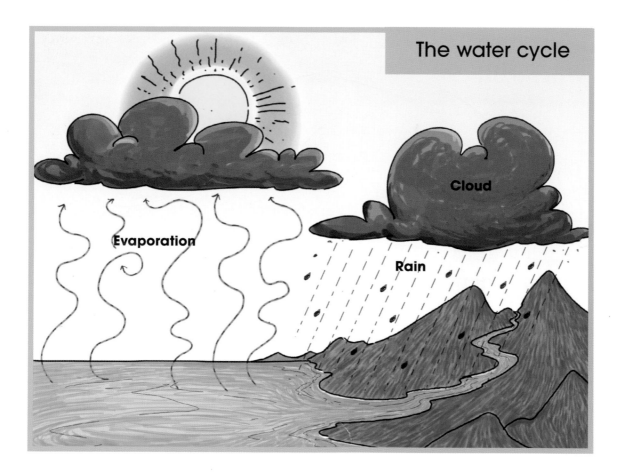

The water cycle

Cloud

Evaporation

Rain

Water all around us

The water on Earth goes round and round in a cycle. It falls on land and sea as rain, sleet or snow. When the Sun warms this water, it **evaporates** and rises into the air to forms clouds. The water falls to the Earth again as rain and collects in lakes, rivers and streams.

Precious water

In hot countries, there is very little water. Water is precious in wet countries, too, because cleaning water costs money and uses **energy**. We can care for the planet by not wasting clean water that pours from our taps. We should only take the water that we need.

■ Water is cleaned at a water treatment plant.

Save water when you clean your teeth

1 Leave the tap running while you clean your teeth for 1 minute.

2 Collect this running water in a washing-up bowl and measure it in a jug. It should be about 3 litres.

3 Use this water to wash your hands, to water plants or to fill a bird-bath.

How many people live in your home? If they turn off the tap every time they clean their teeth, how much clean water will your household save?

Where I live

Do you live in a big city or a tiny village? Wherever you live, you can make your area a better place for the people, plants and animals that live there.

This garden used to be a patch of grass. This family have found lots of ways to improve it.

Welcoming wildlife

If you have a garden or window box, you can plant flowers to attract bees and butterflies. An area full of plant life encourages birds, small animals and insects to visit. A tree helps to keep the air clean.

How could your area be improved?

1 Draw a plan of the area around your home (A). Include features such as buildings, roads, parks, pedestrian crossings and car parks.

2 Ask the following questions:

a) Is it a good place for people, plants and animals to live?

b) Is it clean and safe?

c) How could it be improved?

3 Now draw the plan again, adding features that you think would improve the area (B).

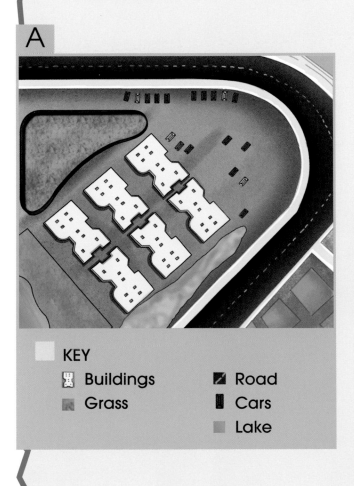

A

KEY

🏢 Buildings   ▨ Road

▨ Grass   ▮ Cars

▨ Lake

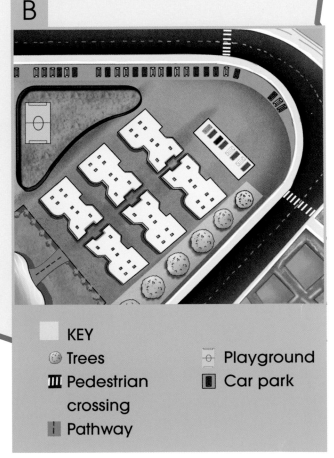

B

KEY

🌳 Trees   Playground

Ⅲ Pedestrian crossing   🅿 Car park

▮ Pathway

Travelling around

We can care for the planet by the way we choose to travel around. Cars, buses and trucks burn fossil fuels that pollute the air with **carbon emissions**.

Short journeys

For short journeys it is easy to walk or cycle. These forms of exercise help to keep us fit. Walking and cycling are good for the planet, too, because they don't use fossil fuels. They are useful ways to travel around without causing **pollution**.

If you walk or cycle to school, you use your own energy to move.

Long journeys

For longer journeys we need to use cars, buses, trains or planes. Using public transport and sharing lifts helps to reduce the number of vehicles that are used and cuts pollution and carbon emissions.

Buses carry lots of people. They help to save many car journeys.

Choose the best journey to school

1 Find out the distance between your home and your school.

2 How long does the journey take:
by foot
by bike
by bus
by car?

3 Which journeys are good for your health?

4 Which journeys are bad for the planet?

Collect information about your journey to school and create a chart like the one shown below.

Distance 1.2 km	Time	Good for planet	Good for me	Comments
Walk	25 minutes	*****	*****	fun – in good weather
Cycle	12 minutes	*****	*****	cycle lanes essential
Bus	10 minutes	***	–	don't miss the bus!
Car	5 minutes	–	–	nowhere to park but very quick!

Litter

Litter is any rubbish that hasn't been thrown away in a bin or **recycled**. Litter is dirty and can be dangerous to wildlife.

The pollution in this river is a threat to plant and animal life.

The effects of litter

Some animals mistake litter for food. They can choke on it or be poisoned. Other animals get trapped in rubbish. Broken glass may cut them. Litter in the street gets washed down drains where it flows into rivers and the sea. It can pollute the water, block pipes and cause flooding.

Litter at school

Children who keep their school playground free of litter set a good example to others. Litter bins, recycling schemes, litter picks and poster campaigns can all help to make a difference.

This playground is full of litter.

Teachers and pupils help to keep this playground clean.

Design an anti-litter poster

Think of a poster that would make everyone at your school stop and think before leaving litter.

1 What do you want your poster to say?

2 What words and picture will say it for you?

3 Use strong, bright colours and short, catchy phrases.

Don't litter the planet!

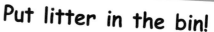

Put litter in the bin!

Reduce, re-use!

The things we use are made of **materials**. Our socks are made of cotton, for example. The paper in this book comes from wood and the pens we write with are made of plastic.

Renewable and non-renewable

Some materials are **renewable**. Cotton and wood, for example, can be grown and replaced. Other materials such as metal and plastic (which is made from oil) are **non-renewable**. One day these materials will run out.

■ You could sort the things you use at school into renewable and non-renewable materials.

Think before you throw!

We throw away all kinds of things that could be used again. Making the most of materials is a good way of saving the planet's resources. If you no longer want something, you could always give it to someone else to use.

You could mend, embroider or decorate your clothes to give them a new life instead of throwing them away.

Re-use paper to make a notepad

1 Take a small cardboard box. Cut off the lid and part of one of the sides and decorate the box.

2 Collect paper that has only been used on one side.

3 Cut the paper into smaller pieces so it fits in the box (clean side up).

4 Punch a hole in the side of the box. Tie a pencil or pen on a piece of string and attach it to the box.

Put your pad by the telephone for notes or in the kitchen for shopping lists. Keep it topped up with used paper.

Recycle!

If you can't re-use something, you may be able to recycle it instead of throwing it away. Recycling means using the materials that objects are made from to make something new.

Rubbish!

Rubbish has to go somewhere. It is usually recycled, burned or buried in a **landfill site**. Burying our rubbish keeps it out of sight while it **rots**, but we are running out of places to put it. Today we can recycle many materials, including paper, plastic, metal and glass.

Recycling helps to cut down rubbish and saves the energy used to make new materials.

Organic and inorganic

Organic materials come from things that were once alive. Examples include food (from plants and animals) and paper (from wood). **Inorganic** materials, such as glass, metal and plastic, have not been alive.

Organic materials rot and decay. They can be turned into compost and dug back into the soil.

Find out how rubbish decays

You will need:
- 2 buckets
- soil and leaves
- 2 cloths

1 Collect rubbish from school packed lunches. Sort it into:
 a) Organic materials (such as apple cores, banana peel, crusts of bread)
 b) Inorganic materials (such as plastic pots, drinks cans, glass bottles)

2 Bury the inorganic rubbish in one bucket of soil and leaves. Bury the organic rubbish in another bucket of soil and leaves.

3 Water both buckets lightly and cover them with a cloth.

4 After about 8 weeks you should find that only the organic material has rotted into the soil.

Pollution

Pollution is harmful dirt that gets into the air, soil and water. We can help care for the planet by keeping the environment free of pollution.

Smog hangs over this city on a hot sunny day.

Smog

In big cities on sunny days, the exhaust fumes from vehicles can combine with the air to form **smog**. Smog is a mixture of smoke and fog. It is like a thick, dirty cloud. Using public transport to cut exhaust fumes from cars is one way to reduce smog levels.

Dirty water

Chemicals, plastics and metals do not rot very easily. It they are thrown away carelessly, they can pollute streams and rivers that flow into the sea. This pollution can harm plants and animals and makes our drinking water dirty.

Monitor air pollution

You will need:
- scissors • five large squares of light-coloured cloth
- five small squares of dark-coloured cloth • glue stick

1 Cut one of the small pieces of cloth into a leaf shape.

2 Lightly glue your leaf-shaped cloth to the middle of a large piece of cloth.

3 Hang the two pieces of cloth outside – by a window or a place sheltered from rain.

4 After a week or more, pull the pieces of cloth apart. You should find that the small cloth leaves a leaf shape in the middle of the large cloth. Pollution in the air will have made the exposed cloth dirty.

5 Try the activity a few more times with new pieces of cloth, hanging the cloths in different places to see which areas are most polluted.

Local wildlife

Wherever we live, we share our local area with other animals. Farming, buildings and roads change the environment. They make it difficult for wildlife to find food and shelter.

A city park is a space that can be shared by people and local wildlife.

City life

We can care for the planet by helping to make our local area a good place for wildlife as well as people. Cities are built for people to live and work in but they are home to plants and animals, too.

Countryside

In the countryside there is plenty of green space, but animals can still be threatened. Fields of crops are sprayed with poisonous **pesticides**. On some farms, fences and cages prevent animals from roaming freely and finding food.

The chickens on this farm are free to move around.

Make a bird station

Help encourage local wildlife with a bird station.

1 Hang a bird feeder on a branch or pole.

2 Put out a bowl of water nearby for drinking and for a bird-bath.

3 Keep a record of the birds that visit your bird station.

sparrow – ̶N̶H̶ ̶N̶H̶ ̶N̶H̶

blue tit – ̶N̶H̶ ̶N̶H̶ ̶N̶H̶ ̶N̶H̶ ̶N̶H̶

Habitats

Deserts, mountains, rainforests and the seashore are all **habitats**. They are home to particular plants and animals. We need to look after these habitats to make sure that all the plants and creatures survive.

As the Earth gets warmer, icebergs melt and polar animals lose their habitat.

Changing habitats

Global warming is changing some habitats and putting the plants and animals that live there at risk. As the Earth warms, rivers dry up, plants die and animals have no water to drink.

Coral reef

Coral reefs take a long time to grow. They are home to many ocean plants and animals. They shelter coastal waters and protect the mainland from storm waves.

Global warming makes the sea too warm for coral reefs to survive. This puts other plants and animals at risk.

Adopt an animal

1 Ask an adult to help you use the Internet to research how to adopt an animal. The website www.adoption.co.uk has lots of animals to choose from. Orang-utans, for example, are endangered because the forests they live in are being cut down. The money you give can help to save the forests and the orang-utans.

2 Think of how you can raise some money for your adopted animal. You could perhaps hold a 'bring and buy' sale and recycle unwanted things at the same time.

Energy

Energy is the power that makes things work.
At home, we use a type of energy called
electricity to work our lights, televisions,
washing machines and fridges.

Strong sea breezes turn the blades of these wind turbines to generate electricity.

Saving energy

We burn fossil fuels to release energy. We need to use this
energy carefully because fossil fuels are running out. We
also need to reduce the carbon emissions they produce.
At home, we can turn off lights and turn down the heating
to save energy. In the future, we need to find energy
sources that will not run out. The Sun, the wind and water
are all types of renewable energy that cause less pollution.

Make a windsock

You will need:
- strip of card 30 cm x 8 cm
- plastic bag cut into a 30 x 30 cm square • stapler
- hole puncher • string • paper clip • garden cane (about 1.5 metres tall) • sticky tape

1 Punch three holes 10 cm apart along the long edge of the card.

2 Cut the plastic square into strips, leaving an uncut strip at the top. Staple to the long card edge without the holes.

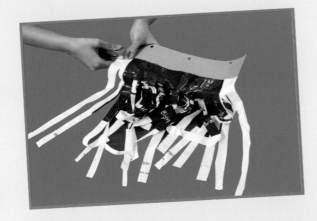

3 Join the ends of the card together to make a cylinder and staple securely.

4 Tie three pieces of string, 20 cm long, to the three holes and tie these to a paper clip.

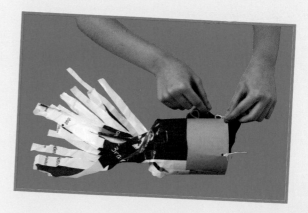

5 Tie the paper clip to a piece of string 60 cm long and tape this to the top of a garden cane. Fix the cane in the ground.

You can tell the strength of the wind by the height of your windsock. What might be good about wind power? What might be bad?

Glossary

carbon emissions

Carbon emissions are gases containing carbon that are sent into the air when we burn fossil fuels such as coal, oil and gas.

coral reef

A coral reef is a ridge of living coral growing on top of coral skeletons. A coral reef lies just below the water in warm seas.

electricity

Electricity is a kind of energy. We use electricity in our homes and schools to give us light and to work machines.

energy

Energy is the force that makes things move, heat up or change.

evaporates

Water evaporates when it heats up and changes from a liquid into a gas called water vapour. This change is called evaporation.

fossil fuel

A fossil fuel is a type of fuel that contains carbon. Fossil fuels release carbon into the air when they are burned.

global warming

Global warming is the rise in the Earth's temperature. It is partly caused by a build-up of gases in the air when we burn fossil fuels.

habitat

A habitat is the natural surrounding that is home to an animal or a plant. For example, the desert is the habitat of a cactus plant.

inorganic

Inorganic materials are materials that have never been alive. Metal and glass are inorganic materials.

landfill site

A landfill site is a huge pit in the ground where rubbish is buried.

materials

Materials are the different substances that are used to make the things around us.

non-renewable

Non-renewable energy or materials cannot be replaced. When they are used up, they are gone forever.

organic

Organic materials were once alive. Compost, made from rotten leaves and vegetables, is organic.

pesticide

A pesticide is made up of chemicals. It is used to kill pests, such as insects, that damage crops.

pollution

Pollution is caused when something harmful or dirty goes into the air, soil or water. For example, carbon emissions pollute the air.

recycle

To recycle means to break something down and re-use the materials to make something new.

renewable

Things that are renewable can be replaced because they can be made again and will not run out. Solar energy is renewable because energy from the Sun will never run out.

rot

Rot means to break down. When organic materials rot, they break down and become part of the soil.

smog

Smog is a type of air pollution. It is caused on hot, sunny days when pollution, such as the exhaust fumes from vehicles, combines with the air to form a thick cloud.

Index